www.providencebooks.net

Publisher Contact

Email:contact@providencebooks.net

Social media: facebook.com/providencebooks

Acknowledgements

The team at Providence Books would like to thank our friends, family, suppliers and customers for making our vision of creating the highest-quality books a reality. Thanks for purchasing and enjoy the quotes!

This page is intentionally left blank

This page is intentionally left blank

A hallucination is a fact, not an error; what is erroneous is a judgment based upon it.

Bertrand Russell

A happy life must be to a great extent a quiet life, for it is only in an atmosphere of quiet that true joy dare live.

Bertrand Russell

A life without adventure is likely to be unsatisfying, but a life in which adventure is allowed to take whatever form it will is sure to be short.

Bertrand Russell

A process which led from the amoeba to man appeared to the philosophers to be obviously a progress though whether the amoeba would agree with this opinion is not known.

Bertrand Russell

A sense of duty is useful in work but offensive in personal relations. People wish to be liked, not to be endured with patient resignation.

Bertrand Russell

A truer image of the world, I think, is obtained by picturing things as entering into the stream of time from an eternal world outside, than from a view which regards time as the devouring tyrant of all that is.

Bertrand Russell

Admiration of the proletariat, like that of dams, power stations, and aeroplanes, is part of the ideology of the machine age.

Bertrand Russell

Advocates of capitalism are very apt to appeal to the sacred principles of liberty, which are embodied in one maxim: The fortunate must not be restrained in the exercise of tyranny over the unfortunate.

Bertrand Russell

Against my will, in the course of my travels, the belief that everything worth knowing was known at Cambridge gradually wore off. In this respect my travels were very useful to me.

Bertrand Russell

All movements go too far.

Bertrand Russell

Almost everything that distinguishes the modern world from earlier centuries is attributable to science, which achieved its most spectacular triumphs in the seventeenth century.

Bertrand Russell

Anything you're good at contributes to happiness.

Bertrand Russell

Aristotle could have avoided the mistake of thinking that women have fewer teeth than men, by the simple device of asking Mrs. Aristotle to keep her mouth open while he counted.

Bertrand Russell

Aristotle maintained that women have fewer teeth than men; although he was twice married, it never occurred to him to verify this statement by examining his wives' mouths.

Bertrand Russell

Awareness of universals is called conceiving, and a universal of which we are aware is called a concept.

Bertrand Russell

Boredom is... a vital problem for the moralist, since half the sins of mankind are caused by the fear of it.

Bertrand Russell

Both in thought and in feeling, even though time be real, to realise the unimportance of time is the gate of wisdom.

Bertrand Russell

Collective fear stimulates herd instinct, and tends to produce ferocity toward those who are not regarded as members of the herd.

Bertrand Russell

Contempt for happiness is usually contempt for other people's happiness, and is an elegant disguise for hatred of the human race.

Bertrand Russell

Conventional people are roused to fury by departure from convention, largely because they regard such departure as a criticism of themselves.

Bertrand Russell

Democracy is the process by which people choose the man who'll get the blame.

Bertrand Russell

Do not fear to be eccentric in opinion, for every opinion now accepted was once eccentric.

Bertrand Russell

Dogmatism and skepticism are both, in a sense, absolute philosophies; one is certain of knowing, the other of not knowing. What philosophy should dissipate is certainty, whether of knowledge or ignorance.

Bertrand Russell

Drunkenness is temporary suicide.

Bertrand Russell

Ethics is in origin the art of recommending to others the sacrifices required for cooperation with oneself.

Bertrand Russell

Every philosophical problem, when it is subjected to the necessary analysis and justification, is found either to be not really philosophical at all, or else to be, in the sense in which we are using the word, logical.

Bertrand Russell

Extreme hopes are born from extreme misery.

Bertrand Russell

Fear is the main source of superstition, and one of the main sources of cruelty. To conquer fear is the beginning of wisdom.

Bertrand Russell

Freedom comes only to those who no longer ask of life that it shall yield them any of those personal goods that are subject to the mutations of time.

Bertrand Russell

Freedom in general may be defined as the absence of obstacles to the realization of desires.

Bertrand Russell

Freedom of opinion can only exist when the government thinks itself secure.

Bertrand Russell

I believe in using words, not fists. I believe in my outrage knowing people are living in boxes on the street. I believe in honesty. I believe in a good time. I believe in good food. I believe in sex.

Bertrand Russell

I do not pretend to start with precise questions. I do not think you can start with anything precise. You have to achieve such precision as you can, as you go along.

Bertrand Russell

I like mathematics because it is not human and has nothing particular to do with this planet or with the whole accidental universe - because, like Spinoza's God, it won't love us in return.

Bertrand Russell

I remain convinced that obstinate addiction to ordinary language in our private thoughts is one of the main obstacles to progress in philosophy.

Bertrand Russell

I say quite deliberately that the Christian religion, as organized in its Churches, has been and still is the principal enemy of moral progress in the world.

Bertrand Russell

I think we ought always to entertain our opinions with some measure of doubt. I shouldn't wish people dogmatically to believe any philosophy, not even mine.

Bertrand Russell

I would never die for my beliefs because I might be wrong.

Bertrand Russell

I've made an odd discovery. Every time I talk to a savant I feel quite sure that happiness is no longer a possibility. Yet when I talk with my gardener, I'm convinced of the opposite.

Bertrand Russell

If all our happiness is bound up entirely in our personal circumstances it is difficult not to demand of life more than it has to give.

Bertrand Russell

If any philosopher had been asked for a definition of infinity, he might have produced some unintelligible rigmarole, but he would certainly not have been able to give a definition that had any meaning at all.

Bertrand Russell

If there were in the world today any large number of people who desired their own happiness more than they desired the unhappiness of others, we could have a paradise in a few years.

Bertrand Russell

In America everybody is of the opinion that he has no social superiors, since all men are equal, but he does not admit that he has no social inferiors, for, from the time of Jefferson onward, the doctrine that all men are equal applies only upwards, not downwards.

Bertrand Russell

In all affairs it's a healthy thing now and then to hang a question mark on the things you have long taken for granted.

Bertrand Russell

In the revolt against idealism, the ambiguities of the word experience have been perceived, with the result that realists have more and more avoided the word.

Bertrand Russell

Indignation is a submission of our thoughts, but not of our desires.

Bertrand Russell

It has been said that man is a rational animal. All my life I have been searching for evidence which could support this.

Bertrand Russell

It is possible that mankind is on the threshold of a golden age; but, if so, it will be necessary first to slay the dragon that guards the door, and this dragon is religion.

Bertrand Russell

It is preoccupation with possessions, more than anything else, that prevents us from living freely and nobly.

Bertrand Russell

It seems to be the fate of idealists to obtain what they have struggled for in a form which destroys their ideals.

Bertrand Russell

Italy, and the spring and first love all together should suffice to make the gloomiest person happy.

Bertrand Russell

Liberty is the right to do what I like; license, the right to do what you like.

Bertrand Russell

Life is nothing but a competition to be the criminal rather than the victim.

Bertrand Russell

Love is something far more than desire for sexual intercourse; it is the principal means of escape from the loneliness which afflicts most men and women throughout the greater part of their lives.

Bertrand Russell

Machines are worshipped because they are beautiful and valued because they confer power; they are hated because they are hideous and loathed because they impose slavery.

Bertrand Russell

Man is a credulous animal, and must believe something; in the absence of good grounds for belief, he will be satisfied with bad ones.

Bertrand Russell

Man needs, for his happiness, not only the enjoyment of this or that, but hope and enterprise and change.

Bertrand Russell

Many a man will have the courage to die gallantly, but will not have the courage to say, or even to think, that the cause for which he is asked to die is an unworthy one.

Bertrand Russell

Many people when they fall in love look for a little haven of refuge from the world, where they can be sure of being admired when they are not admirable, and praised when they are not praiseworthy.

Bertrand Russell

Many people would sooner die than think; in fact, they do so.

Bertrand Russell

Marriage is for women the commonest mode of livelihood, and the total amount of undesired sex endured by women is probably greater in marriage than in prostitution.

Bertrand Russell

Mathematics may be defined as the subject in which we never know what we are talking about, nor whether what we are saying is true.

Bertrand Russell

Mathematics takes us into the region of absolute necessity, to which not only the actual word, but every possible word, must conform.

Bertrand Russell

Men are born ignorant, not stupid. They are made stupid by education.

Bertrand Russell

Men who are unhappy, like men who sleep badly, are always proud of the fact.

Bertrand Russell

Most people would sooner die than think; in fact, they do so.

Bertrand Russell

Much that passes as idealism is disguised hatred or disguised love of power.

Bertrand Russell

Neither a man nor a crowd nor a nation can be trusted to act humanely or to think sanely under the influence of a great fear.

Bertrand Russell

Next to enjoying ourselves, the next greatest pleasure consists in preventing others from enjoying themselves, or, more generally, in the acquisition of power.

Bertrand Russell

No one gossips about other people's secret virtues.

Bertrand Russell

No; we have been as usual asking the wrong question. It does not matter a hoot what the mockingbird on the chimney is singing. The real and proper question is: Why is it beautiful?

Bertrand Russell

None but a coward dares to boast that he has never known fear.

Bertrand Russell

Obscenity is whatever happens to shock some elderly and ignorant magistrate.

Bertrand Russell

Of all forms of caution, caution in love is perhaps the most fatal to true happiness.

Bertrand Russell

One of the symptoms of an approaching nervous breakdown is the belief that one's work is terribly important.

Bertrand Russell

One should respect public opinion insofar as is necessary to avoid starvation and keep out of prison, but anything that goes beyond this is voluntary submission to an unnecessary tyranny.

Bertrand Russell

Order, unity, and continuity are human inventions, just as truly as catalogues and encyclopedias.

Bertrand Russell

Patriotism is the willingness to kill and be killed for trivial reasons.

Bertrand Russell

Patriots always talk of dying for their country and never of killing for their country.

Bertrand Russell

Reason is a harmonising, controlling force rather than a creative one.

Bertrand Russell

Religion is something left over from the infancy of our intelligence, it will fade away as we adopt reason and science as our guidelines.

Bertrand Russell

Religions that teach brotherly love have been used as an excuse for persecution, and our profoundest scientific insight is made into a means of mass destruction.

Bertrand Russell

Religions, which condemn the pleasures of sense, drive men to seek the pleasures of power. Throughout history power has been the vice of the ascetic.

Bertrand Russell

Right discipline consists, not in external compulsion, but in the habits of mind which lead spontaneously to desirable rather than undesirable activities.

Bertrand Russell

Science is what you know, philosophy is what you don't know.

Bertrand Russell

Sin is geographical.

Bertrand Russell

So far as I can remember, there is not one word in the Gospels in praise of intelligence.

Bertrand Russell

The coward wretch whose hand and heart Can bear to torture aught below, Is ever first to quail and start From the slightest pain or equal foe.

Bertrand Russell

The degree of one's emotions varies inversely with one's knowledge of the facts.

Bertrand Russell

The demand for certainty is one which is natural to man, but is nevertheless an intellectual vice.

Bertrand Russell

The fact that an opinion has been widely held is no evidence whatever that it is not utterly absurd.

Bertrand Russell

The fundamental concept in social science is Power, in the same sense in which Energy is the fundamental concept in physics.

Bertrand Russell

The fundamental defect of fathers, in our competitive society, is that they want their children to be a credit to them.

Bertrand Russell

The good life is one inspired by love and guided by knowledge.

Bertrand Russell

The infliction of cruelty with a good conscience is a delight to moralists. That is why they invented Hell.

Bertrand Russell

The man who can centre his thoughts and hopes upon something transcending self can find a certain peace in the ordinary troubles of life, which is impossible to the pure egoist.

Bertrand Russell

The megalomaniac differs from the narcissist by the fact that he wishes to be powerful rather than charming, and seeks to be feared rather than loved. To this type belong many lunatics and most of the great men of history.

Bertrand Russell

The most savage controversies are about matters as to which there is no good evidence either way.

Bertrand Russell

The observer, when he seems to himself to be observing a stone, is really, if physics is to be believed, observing the effects of the stone upon himself.

Bertrand Russell

The only thing that will redeem mankind is cooperation.

Bertrand Russell

The place of the father in the modern suburban family is a very small one, particularly if he plays golf.

Bertrand Russell

The pleasure of work is open to anyone who can develop some specialised skill, provided that he can get satisfaction from the exercise of his skill without demanding universal applause.

Bertrand Russell

The point of philosophy is to start with something so simple as not to seem worth stating, and to end with something so paradoxical that no one will believe it.

Bertrand Russell

The secret of happiness is this: let your interests be as wide as possible, and let your reactions to the things and persons that interest you be as far as possible friendly rather than hostile.

Bertrand Russell

The secret to happiness is to face the fact that the world is horrible.

Bertrand Russell

The slave is doomed to worship time and fate and death, because they are greater than anything he finds in himself, and because all his thoughts are of things which they devour.

Bertrand Russell

The theoretical understanding of the world, which is the aim of philosophy, is not a matter of great practical importance to animals, or to savages, or even to most civilised men.

Bertrand Russell

The time you enjoy wasting is not wasted time.

Bertrand Russell

The trouble with the world is that the stupid are cocksure and the intelligent are full of doubt.

Bertrand Russell

The true spirit of delight, the exaltation, the sense of being more than Man, which is the touchstone of the highest excellence, is to be found in mathematics as surely as poetry.

Bertrand Russell

The universe may have a purpose, but nothing we know suggests that, if so, this purpose has any similarity to ours.

Bertrand Russell

The whole problem with the world is that fools and fanatics are always so certain of themselves, and wiser people so full of doubts.

Bertrand Russell

The world is full of magical things patiently waiting for our wits to grow sharper.

Bertrand Russell

There is much pleasure to be gained from useless knowledge.

Bertrand Russell

There is no need to worry about mere size. We do not necessarily respect a fat man more than a thin man. Sir Isaac Newton was very much smaller than a hippopotamus, but we do not on that account value him less.

Bertrand Russell

There is something feeble and a little contemptible about a man who cannot face the perils of life without the help of comfortable myths.

Bertrand Russell

Those who forget good and evil and seek only to know the facts are more likely to achieve good than those who view the world through the distorting medium of their own desires.

Bertrand Russell

Those who have never known the deep intimacy and the intense companionship of mutual love have missed the best thing that life has to give.

Bertrand Russell

Thought is subversive and revolutionary, destructive and terrible, Thought is merciless to privilege, established institutions, and comfortable habit. Thought is great and swift and free.

Bertrand Russell

Three passions, simple but overwhelmingly strong, have governed my life: the longing for love, the search for knowledge, and unbearable pity for the suffering of mankind.

Bertrand Russell

To acquire immunity to eloquence is of the utmost importance to the citizens of a democracy.

Bertrand Russell

To be without some of the things you want is an indispensable part of happiness.

Bertrand Russell

To conquer fear is the beginning of wisdom.

Bertrand Russell

To fear love is to fear life, and those who fear life are already three parts dead.

Bertrand Russell

To teach how to live without certainty and yet without being paralysed by hesitation is perhaps the chief thing that philosophy, in our age, can do for those who study it.

Bertrand Russell

To understand a name you must be acquainted with the particular of which it is a name.

Bertrand Russell

War does not determine who is right - only who is left.

Bertrand Russell

We are faced with the paradoxical fact that education has become one of the chief obstacles to intelligence and freedom of thought.

Bertrand Russell

What is wanted is not the will to believe, but the will to find out, which is the exact opposite.

Bertrand Russell

When the intensity of emotional conviction subsides, a man who is in the habit of reasoning will search for logical grounds in favour of the belief which he finds in himself.

Bertrand Russell

Why is propaganda so much more successful when it stirs up hatred than when it tries to stir up friendly feeling?

Bertrand Russell

With the introduction of agriculture mankind entered upon a long period of meanness, misery, and madness, from which they are only now being freed by the beneficent operation of the machine.

Bertrand Russell

Work is of two kinds: first, altering the position of matter at or near the earth's surface relative to other matter; second, telling other people to do so.

Bertrand Russell

This page is intentionally left blank

This page is intentionally left blank

This page is intentionally left blank

This page is intentionally left blank

This page is intentionally left blank

www.ingramcontent.com/pod-product-compliance
Lightning Source LLC
Chambersburg PA
CBHW061933280526
45787CB00004B/1591